YOUR KNOWLEDGE HAS VALUE

- We will publish your bachelor's and master's thesis, essays and papers

- Your own eBook and book - sold worldwide in all relevant shops

- Earn money with each sale

Upload your text at www.GRIN.com
and publish for free

Bibliographic information published by the German National Library:

The German National Library lists this publication in the National Bibliography; detailed bibliographic data are available on the Internet at http://dnb.dnb.de .

This book is copyright material and must not be copied, reproduced, transferred, distributed, leased, licensed or publicly performed or used in any way except as specifically permitted in writing by the publishers, as allowed under the terms and conditions under which it was purchased or as strictly permitted by applicable copyright law. Any unauthorized distribution or use of this text may be a direct infringement of the author s and publisher s rights and those responsible may be liable in law accordingly.

Imprint:

Copyright © 2014 GRIN Verlag, Open Publishing GmbH
Print and binding: Books on Demand GmbH, Norderstedt Germany
ISBN: 9783668432994

This book at GRIN:

http://www.grin.com/en/e-book/358719/changes-using-music-to-explore-post-war-british-youth-culture

Lindsey McIntosh

"Changes". Using music to explore post-war British youth culture

GRIN Publishing

GRIN - Your knowledge has value

Since its foundation in 1998, GRIN has specialized in publishing academic texts by students, college teachers and other academics as e-book and printed book. The website www.grin.com is an ideal platform for presenting term papers, final papers, scientific essays, dissertations and specialist books.

Visit us on the internet:

http://www.grin.com/

http://www.facebook.com/grincom

http://www.twitter.com/grin_com

Q. 'How significant is music to an understanding of youth culture in post-war Britain?'

'And these children that you spit on as they try to change their worlds,
Are immune to your consultations – they're quite aware of what they're going through...'

- David Bowie, 'Changes' [*Hunky Dory*, 1971]

When the American director John Hughes chose to open the credits of his 1985 film *The Breakfast Club* with these lyrics taken from David Bowie's 1971 single 'Changes', his intention in doing so was to challenge the commonplace notions of youth plaguing 1980s teen-culture in America.[1] The film's troubled 'teenage' protagonists, exaggerated caricatures of rebellious youth who spend an entire Saturday detention within a school library in atonement for their individual delinquencies, begin their journey defined 'in the simplest terms and the most convenient definitions' lavished upon them by their adult authorities.[2] Bowie's lyrics were applied to *The Breakfast Club* by Hughes in order to glamorize the notion of 'us versus them' and youth isolation within the cultural landscape of 1980s America. However, these lyrics can also be aptly applied to the much-discussed issue of 'youth culture' within the British post-war landscape. Although 'Changes' was not released until the early 1970s, its lyrics effectively capture the tone of the previous two decades in Britain; decades in the throes of social and political change, with a newly formed 'youth' group who were becoming increasingly aware of that fact. Following the arrival of rock n' roll in the late 1950s, British youths underwent a period of self-realisation in the 1960s as music, particularly rock n' roll, drove a wedge between teenagers and the 'parent culture', effectively isolating them into their own unique cultural island.[3] The primary

---

[1] Loukides, P. and Fuller, L.K. (eds.). *Beyond the Stars: Themes and ideologies in American popular film.* (Popular Press, 1996), p.30.
[2] Hughes, J. *The Breakfast Club.* Universal Pictures, 1985.
[3] Bennett, A. 'Still Talking About My Generation!: The Representation of Youth in Popular Music.' In Jamieson, P. and Romer, D. (eds.). *The Changing Portrayal of Adolescents in the Media Since 1950.* (Oxford: Oxford University Press, 2008), p.60

ambition of this essay, therefore, will be to assess the change implemented by music during these post-war decades and whether it is possible to utilize music as a tool for effectively understanding youth culture and sub-cultures. Although each decade could be argued to embody its own distinct 'mood', effectively captured and echoed in its musical output, this essay will hone its energies primarily towards studying the late 1950s and early 1960s, in which a 'fizzy electrical storm' of a radiant post-war atmosphere was reflected and charged by its music.[4]

In-depth study into the mystified realms of youth culture and its various sub-fractions presents an extremely complex task. Whilst a number of youth-focused historians have approached this subject, an absolute definition surrounding the phrase 'youth culture' still remains predominantly hazy. However, despite engagement with the subject within a variety of different theoretical frameworks, the use of music as a tool for deconstructing and understanding various youth sub-cultural fractions has been largely marginalised in past writings on the subject.[5] Whilst some social historians such as Keith Gildart and Adrian Horn advocate the use of music and its various associations as a useful means of successfully examining British post-war youth culture, others have been equally antagonistic to the idea. One of the key reasons why music is viewed by historians such as F.G. Friedman as an effective means of studying cultural habits of the young is due to its unique association with youth. Writing in *Youth and Society,* Friedman notes that 'music – more perhaps than even drugs or the new awareness of youth in general – constitutes today the dividing line between young and old (across which communication does not seem possible).'[6] Friedman's sentiments are reflected within a modern study conducted in 2000 by Weinstein. Upon

---

[4] MacDonald, I. *Revolution in the Head: The Beatles' Records and the Sixties.* (London: Pimlico, 1998), p.1.
[5] Gildart, K. Images of England Through Popular Music: Class, Youth and Rock 'n' Roll, 1955-1976. (Basingstoke: Palgrave Macmillan, 2013), p.5.
[6] Friedman, F.G. *Youth And Society.* (London: The MacMillan Press Ltd., 1971), p.20.

examining the influence of heavy metal music on its listeners, the study refers to the older generation of fans of this musical genre as 'wistful emigrants', before concluding that their age subsequently excludes them toward fully participating with a 'youthful' genre of music.[7] As these studies help illuminate, the medium of music and certain musical genres are embalmed with youthful properties which helps distinguish 'youth' as a sociocultural category, significantly distinct from older generations.[8] Andy Bennett is but one of the numerous social historians who identifies this link between youth and music, stating that 'since the mid-1950s, popular music has been primarily defined as 'youth' music.'[9] Assertions such as these can be supported by evidence that traces a rise of a distinctive teenage consumer market in the 1950s. In perhaps the most influential study of teenage spending patterns, Mark Abrams' *The Teenage Consumer* (1959) reveals not only were 'affluent' teens the predominant spending group within the British market, but also that their spending was concentrated in particular consumer markets.[10] Identifying a significant 44 per cent of teenage spending to lie concentrated within the music market, whether in purchasing records or record players, Abrams noted that these patterns illustrated the rise of 'distinctive teenage spending for distinctive teenage ends in a distinctive teenage world.'[11] However, in spite of statistical evidence such as Abrams' report, which identifies music as a pivotal source of interest for British youth in the 1950s, some historians continue to consciously trivialise its significance within the field of youth studies. Writing in *Images of England Through Popular Music* (2013), Keith Gildart remarks that despite popular music providing 'a daily soundtrack to a whole generation of English working-class youth in the home, the workplace, coffee bars, pubs, clubs, dance halls and theatres', its utility as a tool

---

[7] Hodkinson, P. and Bennett, A. (eds.). *Ageing and Youth Cultures: Music, Style and Identity*. (Google eBook, 2013) (last accessed: 21/03/14), p.2.
[8] Bennett, A. 'Still Talking About My Generation!: The Representation of Youth in Popular Music.' In Jamieson, P. and Romer, D. (eds.). *The Changing Portrayal of Adolescents in the Media Since 1950*. (Oxford: Oxford University Press, 2008), p.59.
[9] Ibid, p.59.
[10] Osgerby, B. *Youth in Britain since 1945*. (Blackwell Publishers Ltd., 1998), p.24.
[11] Ibid, p.24.

for examining youth culture has been largely overlooked by a number of academic historians.[12] Simon Frith concurs with this, stating that 'academic historians have not been drawn to the field of popular music' as an appropriate instrument for examining the development of youth culture over the past several decades.[13] A primary reason for this marginality within cultural studies is noted by Gildart, who asserts that the elitist education of many 'solidly middle-class academic historians' has led many of them to either 'neglect or belittle aspects of popular culture' as irrelevant.[14] However, Ian MacDonald strongly disagrees with this trivialisation. Whilst admitting the 1960s in Britain were ultimately the product of 'influences deeper than pop' (as both political and economic issues rose to a head in the later course of the decade), he nevertheless highlights the significance of music during this period, remarking that without the vital charge emitted by musicians such as The Beatles, the 'fizzy electrical storm', as described by Liverpool poet Brian Patten, 'might have hardly have sparked at all.[15]

In *Images of England*, K. Gildart notes that several historians have often credited 1956 as 'the year when it begins' in Britain.[16] Although the roots of 'rock n' roll' can be traced back to 'folk' music in origin (rhythm and blues-derived music first performed by African American artists such as Fats Domino), it was not until the arrival of white commercial artists such as Bill Haley and Elvis Presley that the beginning of a distinct 'teenage culture' began to unfold on British soil, accompanied by an exciting new

---

[12] Gildart, K. Images of England Through Popular Music: Class, Youth and Rock 'n' Roll, 1955-1976. (Basingstoke: Palgrave Macmillan, 2013), p.2.
[13] Ibid, p.6.
[14] Ibid, p.6.
[15] MacDonald, I. *Revolution in the Head: The Beatles' Records and the Sixties.* (London: Pimlico, 1998), p.1.
[16] Gildart, K. Images of England Through Popular Music: Class, Youth and Rock 'n' Roll, 1955-1976. (Basingstoke: Palgrave Macmillan, 2013), p.14.

soundtrack which reflected this development.[17] Whilst Adrian Horn dedicates a whole book to counteract the myth that British youths were subsequently Americanized during the 1950s and 1960s, he contends that one area in which American influence did successfully penetrate the British psyche is through music. When Bill Haley's 'Rock Around the Clock' was released in Britain in 1956, it topped the British chart and sold over a million copies.[18] The song, whose lyrics essentially conveyed a message of youths having a good time, *all* of the time, indicated a distinct shift away from the parent culture.[19] Larry Birnbaum synonymises the release of 'Rock Around the Clock' with 'the moment rock n' roll exploded in the national consciousness, and also the moment when rock n' roll became firmly associated with youth rebellion.'[20] As the rise of this new genre was still largely misunderstood by the British parent culture, its introduction into Britain caused public concern, owed partially to a perceived connection between 'dangerous' rock n' roll music and juvenile delinquency.[21] Such negative perceptions of rock music were strengthened in part by Hollywood films such as *The Blackboard Jungle*, which displayed images of 'wild, untamed rebel youth' accompanied by soundtracks of exciting and dangerous rock music.[22] The media also played a significant role in shaping these negative assumptions towards 'corrupting' rock music. When the film *Rock Around the Clock* was released in Britain, it marked the beginnings of a 'moral panic.'[23] Although a sociologist report conducted upon youth reactions to the film revealed that little trouble was caused in the majority of cinemas in which the film screened,

---

[17] Bennett, A. 'Still Talking About My Generation!: The Representation of Youth in Popular Music.' In Jamieson, P. and Romer, D. (eds.). *The Changing Portrayal of Adolescents in the Media Since 1950*. (Oxford: Oxford University Press, 2008), p.60.
[18] Horn, A. Juke Box Britain: Americanisation and youth culture, 1945-60. (Manchester: Manchester University Press, 2009), p.78.
[19] Bennett, A. 'Still Talking About My Generation!: The Representation of Youth in Popular Music.' In Jamieson, P. and Romer, D. (eds.). *The Changing Portrayal of Adolescents in the Media Since 1950*. (Oxford: Oxford University Press, 2008), p.61.
[20] Birnbaum, L. *Before Elvis: The Prehistory of Rock n' Roll*. (Rowman & Little, 2013), p.11.
[21] Horn, A. Juke Box Britain: Americanisation and youth culture, 1945-60. (Manchester: Manchester University Press, 2009), p.78.
[22] Ibid, p.78.
[23] Ibid, p.78.

the press reaction was somewhat different.[24] Following the actions of several youths in a South London cinema hall who danced in the cinema aisles, the *Daily Express* claimed that 2,000 young people took to the streets in a collective gathering of teenage rebellion.[25] Media exaggerations such as these helped fan the flames of moral panic amongst the older, 'misunderstanding' generations who denounced the music genre as both 'vulgar and immoral.'[26] Such disproportionate stories were characteristic of both the 1950s and 1960s in Britain, as explored in Stanley Cohen's *Folk Devils and Moral Panics* (1972), in which the author traces the distorting influence of the media in portraying the seaside 'riots' between Mods and Rockers at Clacton in 1964.[27] As incidents such as the *Rock Around the Clock* 'riots' help illuminate, rock music in Britain has always been tarnished with predominantly negative stereotypes. Whilst this does not discredit music's validity as a source for exploring post-war youth culture, it does help show that the subject must be approached with caution, as often what music *actually* represents and what it is *said* to represent appear as two completely different things. Whilst the genre of rock n' roll was branded as 'vulgar' by several officials of the older generation, Andy Bennett remarks essentially it represented 'a fun type of music', used to playfully express feelings of opposition toward 'the mundane day-to-day organization of adult society.'[28] However, the issue of delinquency and 'youth music' proved difficult to divide in the minds of some adult authorities living in post-war Britain, and traces of this mentality have trickled through the subsequent decades into modern-day society. An updated model of negative attitudes towards music today can be sourced within the surplus of studies conducted in attempt to prove links between rap music and youth violence, as it is

---

[24] Ibid, p.79.
[25] Ibid, p.79.
[26] Birnbaum, L. *Before Elvis: The Prehistory of Rock n' Roll*. (Rowman & Little, 2013), p.11.
[27] Cohen, Stanley. *Folk Devils and Moral Panics*. (Taylor & Francis, 2011), p.163.
[28] Bennett, A. 'Still Talking About My Generation!: The Representation of Youth in Popular Music.' In Jamieson, P. and Romer, D. (eds.). *The Changing Portrayal of Adolescents in the Media Since 1950.* (Oxford: Oxford University Press, 2008), p.61.

frequently argued that rap 'causes' or 'contributes to' negative youth behaviour.[29] As a result of such distortions concerning music's influence over young persons, both past and present, other factors such as the influence of the media should perhaps also be studied in relation with music in order to generate an appropriately balanced view of youth culture.

Following Haley's success with the Comets in 1956, various other American artists were able to implement their presence in the British music charts during the late 1950s. Mark Donnelly identifies Elvis Presley in particular as having been a 'towering force' in the British music business, holding 'a virtual monopoly on the international male singer and personality awards in the New Musical Express readers' polls during the 1960s.'[30] Despite inspiring a horde of British imitators such as Tommy Steele and Cliff Richard, Stuart Hall and Paddy Whannel assert that 'no British singer has ever been able to match Presley's musical energy.'[31] Whilst this may appear a subjective statement, it is an accurate reflection of the impact that the aptly named 'King' had upon British youth audiences. When Presley sang about love and heartache, Bennett notes it was with a 'rawness and sensuality that resonated intimately with the teenage psyche.'[32] It was in correlation with the arrival of Elvis Presley that rock n' roll was revealed to British youths as a 'sudden excitement out of nowhere, a cultural force that eclipsed and made irrelevant previous popular music.'[33] Identifying this 'cultural force' to be a teenage passion, Tony Brown attempted to uncover the primary reasons for youths favouring the genre in an article for the *Melody Maker* in

---

[29] Deflem, M. *Popular Culture, Crime and Social Control.* (Emerald Group Publishing, 2010), p.127.
[30] Donnelly, M. *Sixties Britain: Culture, Society and Politics.* (Pearson Education, 2005), p.44.
[31] The Young Audience' in Hall, S. and Whannel, P. (eds.) *The Popular Arts.* (Hutchinson Educational Ltd., 1966 [1964]), p.304.
[32] Bennett, A. 'Still Talking About My Generation!: The Representation of Youth in Popular Music.' In Jamieson, P. and Romer, D. (eds.). *The Changing Portrayal of Adolescents in the Media Since 1950.* (Oxford: Oxford University Press, 2008), p.61.
[33] Makela, J. *John Lennon Imagined: Cultural History of a Rock Star.* (Peter Lang, 2004).

1960.[34] Interviewing a 15-year old male on his attraction to rock music, the young boy replied, 'In our crowd... you have to like rock or you're dead.'[35] Such sentiments were replicated by the majority of youths interviewed for Brown's study. From his findings, Brown was able to conclude that rock music embodied a genre which was 'far more important to [young people] than to adults', as it ultimately helped them to express their independence from an out-dated adult society.[36] As studies such as Brown's illustrate, rock n' roll had become 'a cultural beacon for youth' which helped youngsters to both identify their own distinct social category, and to express it.[37] Further to this, music provided a pivotal means of constructing not only a personal youth identity in the face of stifling adult authority, but also collective youth identities.[38] Youthful themes of 'us versus them' would overspill into the following decade, and would become embedded within the music of the 1960s. The 1965 release of The Who's 'My Generation' reached number two on the singles chart in Britain as it amplified the rebellious vibe of the Sixties counter-culture.[39] Lyrically, it presented not just another song about youth, but a song specifically *for* youth.[40] Candid lyrics such as 'I hope I die before I get old' served as direct attacks to the 'cold' adult generation who were constantly perceived as 'putting them down.'[41]

One of the key reasons why music could be suggested to provide sufficient access to the teenage psyche is due to its strong attachment to other areas of 'teenage' culture. Whilst suggesting that pop and rock music created the distinctive 'teenage' styles of dress

---

[34] Thompson, G. *Please Please Me: Sixties British Pop, Inside Out.* (Oxford: Oxford University Press, 2008), p.29.
[35] Ibid, p.29.
[36] Ibid, p.29.
[37] Bennett, A. 'Still Talking About My Generation!: The Representation of Youth in Popular Music.' In Jamieson, P. and Romer, D. (eds.). *The Changing Portrayal of Adolescents in the Media Since 1950.* (Oxford: Oxford University Press, 2008), p.63.
[38] Ibid, p.74.
[39] Schinder, S. and Schwartz, A. (eds.). *Icons of Rock.* (Greenwood Press, 2008), p.242.
[40] Bennett, A. 'Still Talking About My Generation!: The Representation of Youth in Popular Music.' In Jamieson, P. and Romer, D. (eds.). *The Changing Portrayal of Adolescents in the Media Since 1950.* (Oxford: Oxford University Press, 2008), p.63.
[41] Ibid, p.63.

favoured by post-war British youths would be a wholly inaccurate statement, it would be fair to suggest that it did play a large role in shaping them. When Elvis rose to prominence in Britain during the late 1950s, young male fans attempted to emulate his highly sexualised image. Two decades later, fashion and music were once again seamlessly fused by cross-dressing performers such as David Bowie, whose meta-messages of escape were embedded in equal measure within his musical lyrics and unconventional code of gender-bending dress.[42] Even within a modern context, musical genres have clearly helped influence fashion enormously, with the 2009 Paris fashion show - which saw the haute couture Parisian fashion house of Balmain emulating 'rock chic' through their leather-clad collection - providing just one of many examples.[43] Such instances emphasize the inextricable link between music and fashion since their initial collision in the 1950s. Similarly to music, dress styles have been perceived as powerful instruments of personal expression. This is the case within any age group, but for youths living during the post-war decades in Britain, fashion became a particularly effective tool for externalizing moods of resistance to the parent culture. Further to this, dress is identified by historians such as Bill Osgerby and Dick Hebdige as the most effective means of recognizing post-war subcultural groups. When deteriorated standards of living plagued the British landscape in the late 1970s, the dissonance of the time was reflected by punks not only in their nihilistic soundtracks, but within their raw, antagonistic style of dress also.[44] Although each post-war subcultural group diverge from their contemporaries in terms of style, the uniting focus of their collective dress codes is that it defined itself in opposition to the 'mainstream' culture.[45] Therefore, alongside music, study into sartorial codes of dress should be considered as a valid tool for examining British youth culture, as both of these elements work in harmony with each

---

[42] Ibid, p.67.
[43] Miller, J. *Fashion and Music*. (Berg, 2011), p.1.
[44] Osgerby, B. *Youth in Britain since 1945*. (Blackwell Publishers Ltd., 1998),p.129.
[45] Higgins, M., Smith, C. and Storey, J. (eds.) *The Cambridge Companion to Modern British Culture*. (Cambridge: Cambridge University Press, 2010), p. 213.

other. As they frequently overlap one another within cultural studies, investigating one could provide effective means to understanding the other, contributing to a greater understanding of youth culture overall.

It is perhaps appropriate to end by suggesting that a full understanding of youth culture may never be reached. As music itself is a subjective form, presenting different coded meanings to different individuals, it appears unlikely that the broad scope of 'youth culture' can ever be fully explained or understood simply by using music as an instrument. The 'un-definability' of both 'music' and 'youth culture' are perhaps the reason why these two concepts have become so readily aligned with one another within the field of cultural studies.[46] However, by examining the rebellious lyrics of teenage anthems such as The Who's 'My Generation', it is possible to identify uniquely 'teenage' themes that characterised the changing landscape of post-war Britain. Music also enables the examination of other areas of interest in post-war adolescent life such as fashion, which as this essay has highlighted, holds particularly strong ties with both music and youth culture generally. However, whilst the value of music as a tool for examining youth culture should not be discredited, it should also be approached with caution. As this essay has also briefly explored, the role of the media in the late 1950s and early 1960s played a strong part in casting negative stereotypes upon young people in connection with their musical preferences. Therefore, it is important that attention is paid to the influence of the media when using music as a lens through which youth culture can be examined. To ignore this factor could produce a distorted view of the subject. Overall it can be suggested that music, with its youthful properties and immediate connections to other areas of teenage interest, provides a useful instrument for examining some of the major issues unique to the teenage culture after 1945. However, to produce an accurate reading of youth culture as a whole by

---

[46] Schneck, D.J. and Berger, D. *The Music Effect: Music Physiology and Clinical Applications*. (Jessica Kingsley Publishers, 2005), p.31.

using one factor is practically impossible, as there is no essential 'one-ness' to the subject, no matter what methods are consulted in examining it.[47] Whilst music is a key tool in understanding 'the whole mad modern stew' of post-war Britain, other interrelating ingredients such as fashion and the media must also be included in the study in order to acquire a proper taste of what it really meant to be a teenager in Britain following the Second World War.[48]

---

[47] Donnelly, M. *Sixties Britain: Culture, Society and Politics*. (Pearson Education, 2005). (last accessed 20/03/14), p.5.
[48] Ibid, p.10.

Bibliography

Secondary Sources:

- Bennett, A. 'Still Talking About My Generation!: The Representation of Youth in Popular Music.' In Jamieson, P. and Romer, D. (eds.). *The Changing Portrayal of Adolescents in the Media Since 1950.* (Oxford: Oxford University Press, 2008).

- Birnbaum, L. *Before Elvis: The Prehistory of Rock n' Roll.* (Rowman & Little, 2013).

- Cohen, Stanley. *Folk Devils and Moral Panics.* (Taylor & Francis, 2011).

- Deflem, M. *Popular Culture, Crime and Social Control.* (Emerald Group Publishing, 2010).

- Donnelly, M. *Sixties Britain: Culture, Society and Politics.* (Pearson Education, 2005).

- Friedman, F.G. *Youth And Society.* (London: The MacMillan Press Ltd., 1971).

- Gildart, K. Images of England Through Popular Music: Class, Youth and Rock 'n' Roll, 1955-1976. (Basingstoke: Palgrave Macmillan, 2013).

- Hodkinson, P. and Bennett, A. (eds.). *Ageing and Youth Cultures: Music, Style and Identity.* (Google eBook, 2013) (last accessed: 21/03/14).

- Higgins, M., Smith, C. and Storey, J. (eds.) *The Cambridge Companion to Modern British Culture.* (Cambridge: Cambridge University Press, 2010).

- Horn, A. Juke Box Britain: Americanisation and youth culture, 1945-60. (Manchester: Manchester University Press, 2009).

- Hughes, J. *The Breakfast Club.* Universal Pictures,1985.

- Loukides, P. and Fuller, L.K. (eds.). *Beyond the Stars: Themes and ideologies in American popular film.* (Popular Press, 1996).

- MacDonald, I. *Revolution in the Head: The Beatles' Records and the Sixties.* (London: Pimlico, 1998).

- Makela, J. *John Lennon Imagined: Cultural History of a Rock Star.* (Peter Lang, 2004).

- Miller, J. *Fashion and Music.* (Berg, 2011).

- Osgerby, B. *Youth in Britain since 1945.* (Blackwell Publishers Ltd., 1998).

- Schinder, S. and Schwartz, A. (eds.). *Icons of Rock.* (Greenwood Press, 2008).

- Schneck, D.J. and Berger, D. *The Music Effect: Music Physiology and Clinical Applications.* (Jessica Kingsley Publishers, 2005).

- Thompson, G. *Please Please Me: Sixties British Pop, Inside Out.* (Oxford: Oxford University Press, 2008).

YOUR KNOWLEDGE HAS VALUE

- We will publish your bachelor's and master's thesis, essays and papers

- Your own eBook and book - sold worldwide in all relevant shops

- Earn money with each sale

Upload your text at www.GRIN.com and publish for free